Death of an Empire

Collapse of the Treadwell Gold Mine:

A Pictorial History Book

By Kevin Lee McIver

Published by Groovy Outdoors

www.groovyoutdoors.us/publishing

© 2013 Kevin Lee McIver

http://amzn.com/e/B009QQ7A16

www.mciver.biz

All Rights Reserved.

ISBN-13: 978-1482588309
ISBN-10: 1482588307

Cover photo: The old Treadwell Mine Salt Water Pump House that still stands along the Gastineau Channel on Douglas Island, Alaska. (Photo: Kevin Lee McIver)

Notice: The information in this book is true and complete to the best of our knowledge. It is offered without guarantee on the part of the author or Groovy Outdoors Publishing. The author and Groovy Outdoors Publishing disclaim all liability in conjunction with the use of this book.

No part of this book may be reproduced, stored in a retrieval system, or transmitted by any means without the written permission of the author.

Table of Contents

Prologue

Chapter One – A Brief History   1

Chapter Two – The Treadwell Mine Complex   11

Chapter Three – The Treadwell Miners   57

Chapter Four – Death of the Empire   99

Chapter Five – Treadwell Today   111

Traveling to Alaska   147

Acknowledgements   149

About the Author   151

Bibliography   153

Prologue

In 2011, we steered northwest from Maryland for a job that returned me to Alaska after nearly a decade in the Lower 48—otherwise called "America" by many Alaskans even today. Thoughts of Jack London's Call of the Wild filled our minds and occupied much of our conversation during our trek from urban America into America's Last Frontier. It took many days to clear the United States' border, pass through Canada, cross the famed Yukon, and then drop south by the Alaska Marine Highway ferry from historic Skagway to Juneau—home of the Alaska state capitol.

Within one week after arrival, we selected an interesting trail from a local Trail Mix brochure and headed toward the Treadwell area for a short hike. Little did we realize this was an important area in Alaska's history and the history of gold exploration in America. When we first arrived at the Treadwell Gold Mine Complex on Douglas Island across the Gastineau Channel from Juneau, we were struck by the sheer size of this long gone industrial area. It was as if one stepped back in time to a vast wasteland that was once a mighty gold-producing empire.

Everywhere evidence exists of what was the largest low-grade gold ore mine in the world. Tailings, rusted machinery, concrete structures, decrepit buildings, bits of china along the shore, and tiles from the baths and pool, line the area that extends over a mile south of Douglas. After a dozen or more trips, I realized few outside of local residents know of this historic site and that I had amassed a collection of digital images that would bring to life this story of the Treadwell Empire—it's ultimate collapse—and its fade into history.

I decided to research information about the Treadwell Mines and to ultimately publish this book so others could learn of its fascinating history through a collection of digital photographs and poetry. For Alaskans who have not visited Treadwell and to those longing to visit The Last Frontier—Juneau, Douglas Island, and the Treadwell Mine Complex are the destination to begin your journey.

    Kevin Lee McIver, Author
    Death of an Empire—Collapse of the Treadwell Gold Mine: A Pictorial History

Chapter One – A Brief History

> Gold, gold, we hit the mother lode;
>
> Gold Creek Chief Kowee revealed;
>
> Joe Juneau and Richard Harris struck gold;
>
> The first Alaska stampede was at the Silver Bow.
>
> ♦ ♦ ♦ *Kevin Lee McIver, 2013*

Death of an Empire - Collapse of the Treadwell Gold Mine: A Pictorial History Book

Map of Alaska from the Alaska Juneau Gold Mining Records, 1909. *(Alaska State Library, Alaska Juneau Gold Mining Records, United States Department of the Interior, ASL-M999-AG-04-062-1909)*

Gold was discovered in Alaska a decade before prospectors Joe Juneau and Richard Harris were led by Chief Kowee of the Auk Tlingit who revealed the deposits of gold in the Silver Bow Basin where the city of Juneau was founded that same year in 1880.[1]

This discovery spawned the quest for gold and the surge in mining operations that resulted in the Treadwell Mine on Douglas Island, across the Gastineau Channel from Juneau.[2]

Author of *Treadwell Gold, An Alaska Saga of Riches and Ruin,* Sheila Kelly best describes the Treadwell company mine town as a, "gritty utilitarian settlement boasted an indoor swimming pool, finely-appointed Turkish baths, a clubhouse with movies, dances, billiards, and a library with two thousand books."[3]

Treadwell reached its peak in 1915 when its mills crushed 5,000 tons of ore daily—ore that was valued at $2.50 per ton. The mine was owned and operated by John Treadwell, a carpenter and builder by trade who came to Alaska prior to the Klondike Gold Rush.[4] In 1889, Treadwell sold his stake in the company for $1.5 million and returned to California.[5]

Corporate greed and ill-management resulted in shortcuts taken that reduced the stability of the mines. In 1917 catastrophe struck when waters from the Gastineau Channel flooded three of the

---

[1] The Full Wiki, "Gold Mining in Alaska, Historical lode and placer gold mines, Juneau Mining District," <http://www.thefullwiki.org/Juneau_mining_district>.

[2] City and Borough of Juneau, Parks and Recreation, "History of the Treadwell Mines Alaska," <http://www.juneau.org/parkrec/museum/HTM/Treadwellmine/no/xfeature1.htm>.

[3] Kelly, Sheila, "Treadwell Gold, An Alaska Saga of Riches and Ruin." University of Alaska Press, 2011. <http://www.alaska.edu/uapress/browse/detail/index.xml?id=389>.

[4] Triposo, "Treadwell gold mine," <https://www.triposo.com/poi/N__1006702752>.

[5] Houdek, Jennifer, "Treadwell Gold Mines, 1881-1917," <http://www.litsite.org/index.cfm?section=Digital-Archives&page=Industry&cat=Mining&viewpost=2&ContentId=2743>.

four mines comprising the Treadwell Complex and, "The great enterprise came to a screeching halt."[6] The remaining mine continued to produce ore but ultimately ceased operations in 1922.[7]

Between 1881 and 1922, over 3 million troy ounces of gold were extracted from the mines four sub-sites, earning it the title of the largest hard rock gold mine in the world.[8]

Map of Alaska from the Alaska Juneau Gold Mining Records, 1909*. (Alaska State Library, Alaska Juneau Gold Mining Records, United States Department of the Interior, ASL-M999-AG-04-062-1909)*

---

[6] City and Borough of Juneau, Parks and Recreation, "History of the Treadwell Mines Alaska," <http://www.juneau.org/parkrec/museum/HTM/Treadwellmine/no/xfeature1.htm>.

[7] Stone, David and Brenda, "Golden Places, The History of Alaska-Yukon Mining," <http://www.nps.gov/history/history/online_books/yuch/golden_places/chap7.htm#1> (1980).

[8] Wikipedia, "Treadwell Gold Mine", <http://en.wikipedia.org/wiki/Treadwell_gold_mine>.

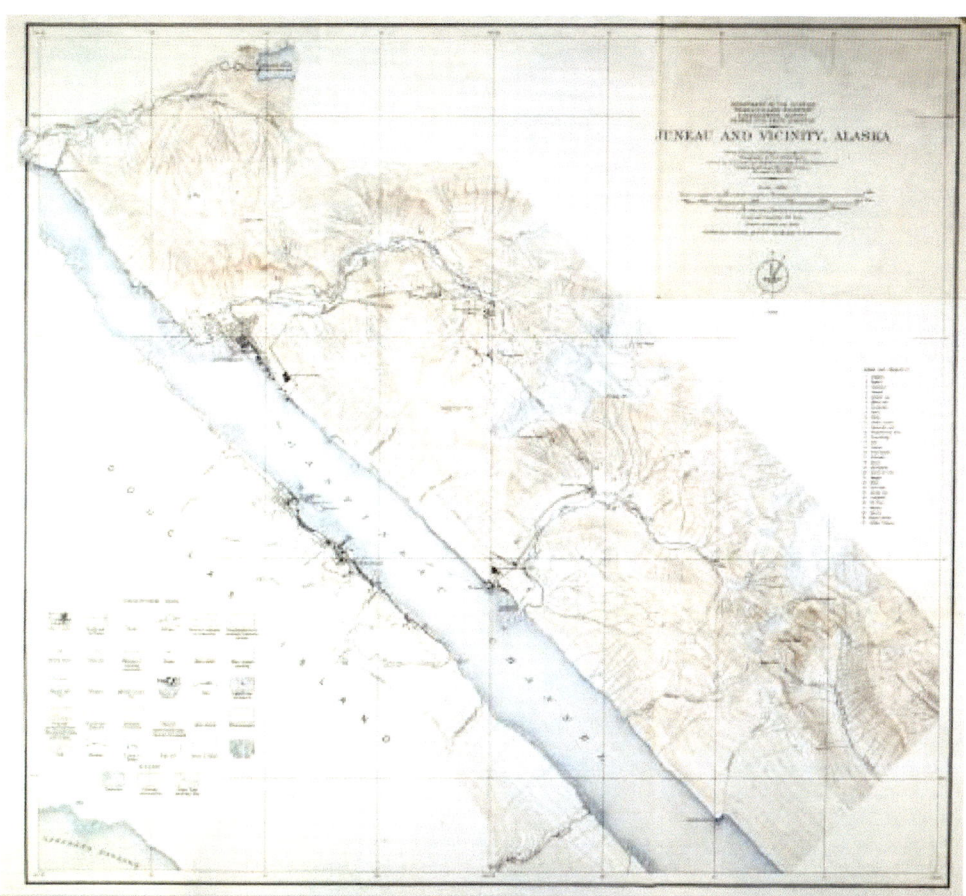

Map of Juneau and vicity, Alaska, Department of the Interior, from survey, 1914-1916. *(Alaska State Library, Alaska State Library Map Case, ASL-G4374-J9C2-1918-G45-MapCase)*

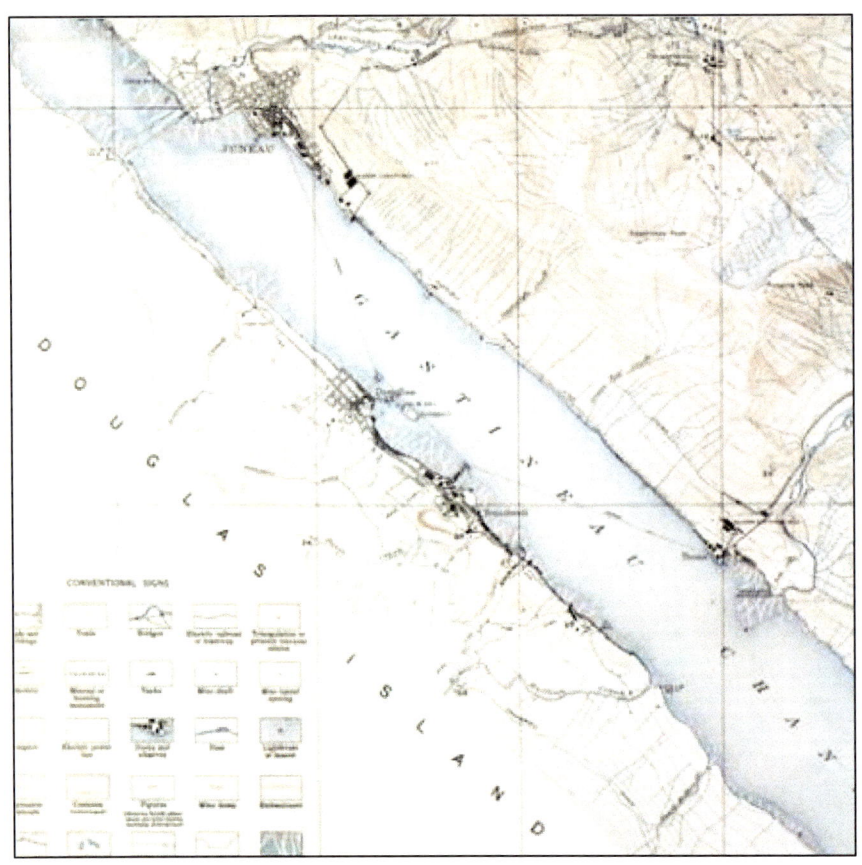

Closer view of the Map of Juneau and vicnity, Alaska, Department of the Interior, from survey, 1914-1916. *The Treadwell Mine Complex is circled in red. (Alaska State Library, Alaska State Library Map Case, ASL-G4374-J9C2-1918-G45-MapCase)*

Indian Village at Juneau in 1887. (Southern Methodist University, Central University Libraries, DeGolyer Library, W.H. Partridge/Partridge's Alaska Photographs.)

Death of an Empire - Collapse of the Treadwell Gold Mine: A Pictorial History Book

Juneau City in 1887. (Southern Methodist University, Central University Libraries, DeGolyer Library, W.H. Partridge/Partridge's Alaska Photographs.)

Panaromic view of Douglas, Alaska, 1914. *Treadwell mine complex is to the right in the photography. (Library of Congress, pan 6a16846)*

Chapter Two – The Treadwell Mine Complex

Wealth rising from the shafts 1800 feet below;

Miners toiled days and nights untold;

But corporate men of greed did not heed;

The many signs of the end were foretold;

From town to empire in two scores;

The deafening mill stamps never more.

♦ ♦ ♦ *Kevin Lee McIver, 2013*

Color postcard of the Treadwell mine company buildings sometime after 1912. (Alaska State Library, William Barquist Collection, ASL-P164-26)

The beginnings of the Treadwell Mine, 1886. *(Alaska State Library, William R. Norton Collection, Photographer: William Howard Case, ASL-P226-306)*

Another view of the mine in 1886. *(Alaska State Library, William R. Norton Collection, Photographer: William Howard Case, ASL-P226-308)*

Residence of the superintendent of the Alaska Treadwell Gold Mining Company, 1898. (Alaska State Library, ASL-P01-1731)

Treadwell Gold Mine Company office, right, and framed attachment on left is the company store, 1896-1913. (Alaska State Library, ASL-P01-1729).

Treadwell Mine buildings, between 1886-1912. (Alaska State Library, Louis L. Stein Collection, ASL-P172-07).

The Glory Hole #5 pit, date unknown. (Alaska State Library, William R. Norton Collection, Case & Draper, ASL-P226-316).

The residence of the Ready Bullion foreman sometime between 1896-1913. (Alaska State Library, Juliane Nick Dexter Collection, 1908, William Howard Case, ASL-P40-10).

Treadwell mine superintendent's house and other mine buildings overlooking the Gastineau Channel, between 1896-1913. (Alaska State Library, Juliane Nick Dexter Collection, 1908, William Howard Case, ASL-P40-15).

Concentrator Floor of the Ready Bullion Mill, sometime between 1896-1899. (Alaska State Library, Winter and Pond Collection, Photographers: Winter and Pond, ASL-P87-0381)

The Treadwell mine boarding house kitchen, west side, between 1896-1913. (Alaska State Library, Case and Draper Collection, Photographers: Case & Draper, ASL-P39-0906.

The assay office grinding room at the Treadwell mine, 1896-1913. (Alaska State Library, Case and Draper Collection, Photographers: Case & Draper, ASL-P39-0945.

A waterfront view of the mining complex sometime between 1896-1913. The area to the left behind the buildings is the famed Glory Hole. (Alaska State Library, Paul Sincic collection, Photographer: Louis H. Pedersen, ASL-P75-417)

Working men's quarters sometime between 1896-1913. (Alaska State Library, Paul Sincic collection, Photographer: Louis H. Pedersen, ASL-P75-423)

The Natatorium at the mine taken sometime between 1890-1913. The swimming pool was complete with diving board and slide. (Alaska State Library, Winter and Pond Collection, ASL-PCA-117).

Looking north toward Juneau. View along left side of beach includes the mine buildings, train trestle, and tracks, taken in 1908. (Alaska State Library, William R. Norton Collection, Photographer: William Howard Case, ASL-P226-313.

Looking along the pier leading to the beach with the Treadwell mine buildings in the background, taken before 1897. (Alaska State Library, Early Prints of Alaska Photograph Collection, ASL-P297-355).

The Ready Bullion Mill Engine Room, date unknown. (Alaska State Library, Winter and Pond Collection, Photographers: Winter & Pond, ASL-P87-1368.

Death of an Empire - Collapse of the Treadwell Gold Mine: A Pictorial History Book

Winter view from the water showing the coal bunkers on the pier, sometime between 1896-1913. (Alaska State Library, William Smith Collection, Photographers: Winter & Pond, ASL-P339-06).

View taken in 1916 above Treadwell Mine looking across the Gastineau Channel toward Juneau. (Alaska State Library, Ed Andrews Collection, Photographer: Ed Andrews, ASL-P162-006)

Treadwell mine buildings lining the waterfront date unknown. (Alaska State Library, William Barquist Collection, ASL-P164-18)

Looking along tracks from Douglas to Treadwell Mine, 1899. (Alaska State Library, William L. Whitaker Collection, ASL-P32-093)

Another view of the superintendent's residence looking toward Juneau taken in 1908. (Alaska State Library, Juliane Nick Dexter Collection, 1908, William Howard Case, ASL-P40-15).

View overlooking the mine looking toward the Gastineau Channel, sometime between 1896-1913. (Alaska State Library, Case and Draper Collection, Photographers: Case & Draper, ASL-P39-0866)

Death of an Empire - Collapse of the Treadwell Gold Mine: A Pictorial History Book

The Mexican Mine operation seen in the foreground looking north, sometime between 1896-1913. (Alaska State Library, Case and Draper Collection, ASL-P39-0956)

Inside the compressor room at the Mexican Mine, date unknown. (Alaska State Library, William R. Norton Collection, Photographers: Case & Draper, ASL-P226-345)

View of the Treadwell wharf and the 700 Mill. (Alaska State Library, William R. Norton Collection, Photographer: William Howard Case, ASL-P226-310)

Looking south along the Gastineau Channel in 1908. (Alaska State Library, William R. Norton Collection, Photographer: William Howard Case, ASL-P226-312)

Death of an Empire - Collapse of the Treadwell Gold Mine: A Pictorial History Book

View of the Treadwell cyanide plant. Taken after 1889. (Alaska State Library, William R. Norton Collection, Photographer: William Howard Case, ASL-P226-317).

View of the new Treadwell foundry taking after 1889. (Alaska State Library, William R. Norton Collection, Photographer: William Howard Case, ASL-P226-318).

Death of an Empire - Collapse of the Treadwell Gold Mine: A Pictorial History Book

View inside the building housing the drill sharpening machines, taken after 1889. (Alaska State Library, William R. Norton Collection, Photographers: Case & Draper, ASL-P226-319.

The Treadwell mine machine shop sometime after 1889. (Alaska State Library, William R. Norton Collection, Photographers: Case & Draper, ASL-P226-310.

The Treadwell Boarding House main dining room taken sometime after 1889. (Alaska State Library, William R. Norton Collection, Photographers: Case & Draper, ASL-P226-325.

Likely this was taken after 1889 inside the Treadwell Amalgamator's room. (Alaska State Library, William R. Norton Collection, Photographers: Case & Draper, ASL-P226-322.

View of the new Treadwell Club Auditorium taken after 1889. (Alaska State Library, William R. Norton Collection, Photographer: William Howard Case, ASL-P226-331).

View of the new Treadwell Club Bowling Alley taken after 1889. (Alaska State Library, William R. Norton Collection, Photographer: William Howard Case, ASL-P226-332).

Death of an Empire - Collapse of the Treadwell Gold Mine: A Pictorial History Book

View of the new New Mexican Boarding House taken after 1889. (Alaska State Library, William R. Norton Collection, Photographer: William Howard Case, ASL-P226-343).

View of the New Mexican boilers that used oil as a fuel source. Taken after 1889. (Alaska State Library, William R. Norton Collection, Photographer: William Howard Case, ASL-P226-348).

The massive 700 Foot Mine hoisting engine. Taken after 1889. (Alaska State Library, William R. Norton Collection, Photographers: Case & Draper, ASL-P226-351).

The massive Mexican Mine old hoisting engine. Taken after 1889. (Alaska State Library, William R. Norton Collection, Photographers: Case & Draper, ASL-P226-347).

Equipment from the 700 Foot Mine, after 1889. (Alaska State Library, William R. Norton Collection, Photographers: Case & Draper, ASL-P226-353).

The Ready Bullion Mine 120 stamp mil, after 1889. (Alaska State Library, William R. Norton Collection, Photographers: Case & Draper, ASL-P226-354).

Inside the Ready Bullion Mine Engine Room, after 1889. (Alaska State Library, William R. Norton Collection, Photographers: Case & Draper, ASL-P226-356).

View of men at the very far end of photo working in Glory Hole at the Treadwell Mine, sometime after 1889. (Alaska State Library, Frank LaRoche Collection, Photographer: Frank LaRoche, ASL-P130-002)

Chapter Three – Treadwell Miners – Life was good

No shanty town like strikes far to the north;

But Treadwell life with comforts akin to back home;

They came for high wages and dreams of gold;

Working in dangerous mines so far below;

On Sunday they dined life in style;

Until the day the mine walls collapsed;

Bringing icy water and the beginning of the past.

♦ ♦ ♦ *Kevin Lee McIver, 2013*

Photo of Robert Allen Kinzie, who served as the assistant superintendent of the Alaska Treadwell Gold Mining, 1900-1905, and general superintendent, 1905-1914. (Alaska State Library, Robert A. Kinzie Photographs, ASL-P13-01)

Treadwell workers outside mine building, ca. 1918. (Alaska State Library, William Barquist Photograph Collection, ASL-P164-24)

The Treadwell Gold Mine 500 foot under the ocean, 1916. (Library of Congress, Frank and Frances Carpenter collection, LC-DIG-ppmsc-02028)

Miners at work underground in 1908. (Alaska State Library, Juliane Nick Dexter Photograph Collection, Photographer: William Howard Case, ASL-P40-19)

Another photo of Treadwell miners in 1908. (Alaska State Library, Juliane Nick Dexter Photograph Collection, Photographer: William Howard Case, ASL-P40-26)

A large group of Treadwell miners in 1908. (Alaska State Library, Juliane Nick Dexter Photograph Collection, Photographer: William Howard Case, ASL-P40-28)

A large group of Treadwell miners posing for a photograph in 1908. Two interesting notes in this photograph include the man in the center is pouring a woman a drink, and on the far right, a man is looking down the sights of a shotgun. (Alaska State Library, Juliane Nick Dexter Photograph Collection, Photographer: William Howard Case, ASL-P40-30)

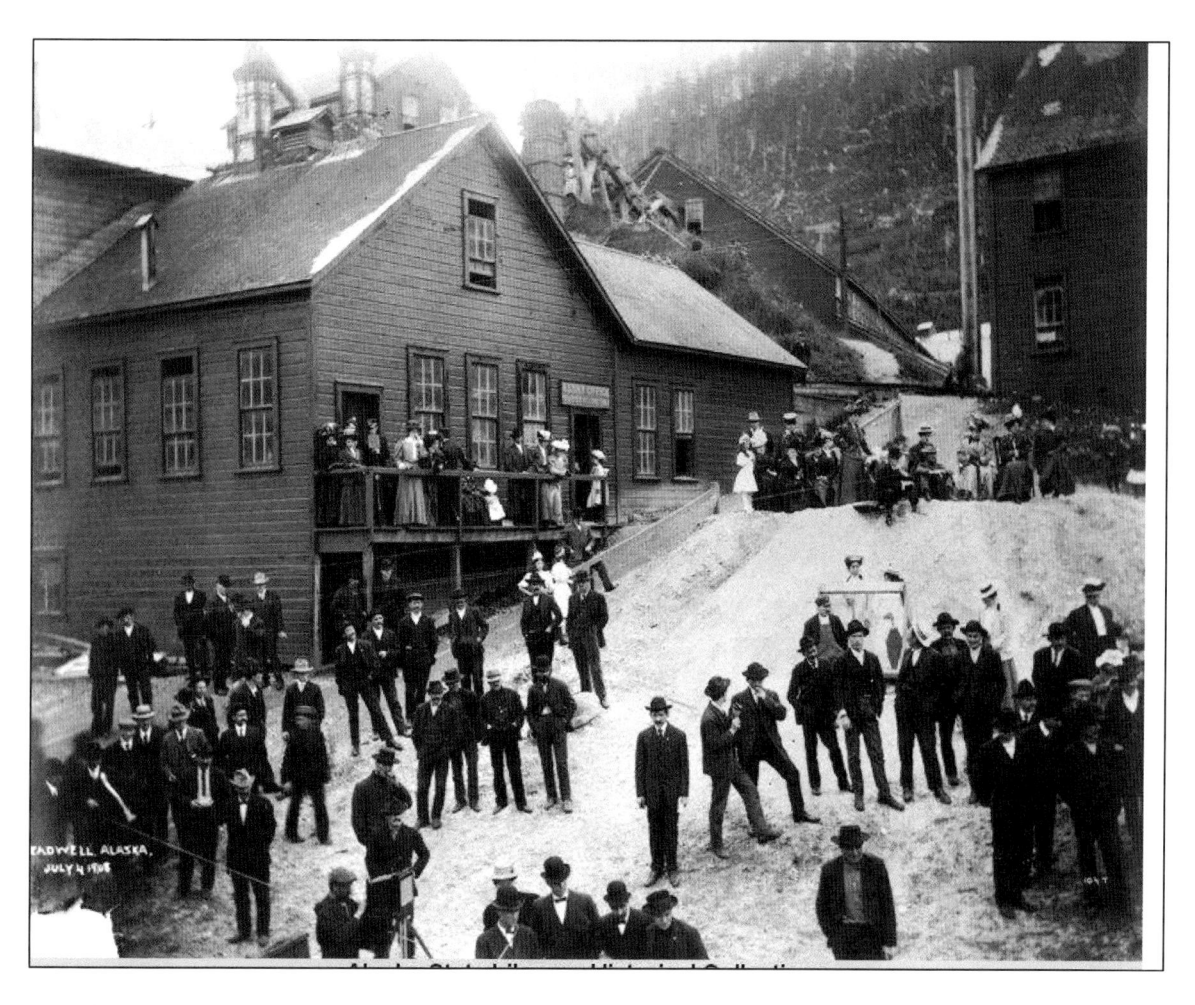

The Fourth of July 1908 at Treadwell. (Alaska State Library, Juliane Nick Dexter Photograph Collection, Photographer: William Howard Case, ASL-P40-32)

Death of an Empire - Collapse of the Treadwell Gold Mine: A Pictorial History Book

Photograph taken in 1907 of men playing pool as volunteer firemen in uniform bearing emblems representing the 700 Mine, Mexican Mine, and the Ready Bullion Mine observe.
(Alaska State Library, Case and Draper Photographs, Photographer: William Howard Case, ASL-P39-0975)

Treadwell employees and officers of the 10th U.S. Infantry. (Alaska State Library, Case and Draper Photographs, Photographers: Case & Draper, ASL-P39-0972)

Treadwell employees and families assembling in area between railroad tracks and mine buildings on July 11, 1908. The Gastineau Channel can be seen in the background. (Alaska State Library, Case and Draper Photographs, Photographers: Case & Draper, ASL-P39-0864)

Treadwell Mine Butcher Shop, sometime between 1898-1920. (Alaska State Library, Case and Draper Photographs, Photographers: Case & Draper, ASL-P39-0896)

Death of an Empire - Collapse of the Treadwell Gold Mine: A Pictorial History Book

The Treadwell Store. Although the only mode of transportation to the Juneau area at that time was by ship, the Treadwell Store featured an abundance of canned goods and fresh fruit.
(Alaska State Library, Case and Draper Photographs, No. 55, PCA 39-1142)

Miners at Treadwell, 1908. (Alaska State Library, Case and Draper Photographs, Photographer: William Howard Case, ASL-P39-0967)

Death of an Empire - Collapse of the Treadwell Gold Mine: A Pictorial History Book

Workers posing for group photograph in 1908. (Alaska State Library, Case and Draper Photographs, Photographer: William Howard Case, ASL-P39-0976)

Group photograph in front of Gastineau Channel, 1908. (Alaska State Library, Case and Draper Photographs, Photographer: William Howard Case, ASL-P39-0979)

Death of an Empire - Collapse of the Treadwell Gold Mine: A Pictorial History Book

Inside the Treadwell Mine General Office. (Alaska State Library, William R. Norton Photograph Collection, Photographers: Case & Draper, ASL-P226-356).

Workers on the Battery Floor, 300 Stamp Mill, ca. 1899. (Alaska State Library, Winter and Pond Photographs, Photographers: Winter and Pond, ASL-P87-0376)

Construction crew posing for a group photograph in 1908. (Alaska State Library, Case and Draper Photographs, Photographer: William Howard Case, ASL-P39-0971)

Worker operating the Treadwell Mine battery-charging switchboard taken sometime after 1912. According to the photo album information, locomotive battery power packs were recharged at the end of each shift. (Alaska State Library, Harry F. Snyder Photograph Collection, Photographer: Harry F. Snyder, ASL-PCA-38)

Treadwell Mine electric locomotives replace horses and mules for hauling ore from the stopes to the station ore bins. (Alaska State Library, Harry F. Snyder Photograph Collection, Photographer: Harry F. Snyder, ASL-P38-020)

Treadwell miners stope mining working on the overhead portion of stope on the 2300 ft. level. Per the album, ore chutes were located on the floor of the tope over an ore train that moved the ore to a bin. From there the ore was hoisted to the surface and fed through crushers at the head of the shaft, and then transported by train to the stamp mills. (Alaska State Library, Harry F. Snyder Photograph Collection, Photographer: Harry F. Snyder, ASL-P38-045)

Workers with the Treadwell express railcar, 1908. (Alaska State Library, Case and Draper Photographs, Photographer: William Howard Case, ASL-P39-0965)

The Ready Bullion hose team and Treadwell Champions, 1914. (Alaska State Library, Ed Andrews Photographs, Photographer: Ed Andrews, ASL-P162-021.)

Treadwell atop the Gyratory Crushing Cone, ca. 1915. (Alaska State Library, William Barquist Photograph Collection, ASL-P164-17)

Treadwell workers operating the Ready Bullion hoist. (Alaska State Library, William Barquist Photograph Collection, ASL-P164-16)

Treadwell Mexican Mine basketball team and champions of Southeast Alaska, 1914. (Alaska State Library, William Barquist Photograph Collection, ASL-P164-25)

Worker atop the 300 Stamp Mill at the Treadwell Mines, sometime between 1896-1913.
(Alaska State Library, John Alexander Stuart Photograph Collection, ASL-P524-12)

Four miners at Treadwell in 1908. (Alaska State Library, Juliane Nick Dexter Photograph Collection, Photographer: William Howard Case, ASL-P40-31)

Group photograph of miners in 1908. (Alaska State Library, Juliane Nick Dexter Photograph Collection, Photographer: William Howard Case, ASL-P40-27)

Miners with drill and other equipment at the 1500 ft. level of the Ready Bullion Mine, 1908.
(Alaska State Library, Juliane Nick Dexter Photograph Collection, Photographer: William Howard Case, ASL-P40-21)

Workers inserting potatoes into the Economical Vegetable Peeling Machine manufactured by Belding & Franklin of New York, NY. (Alaska State Library, Case and Draper Photographs, Photographers: Case & Draper, ASL-P39-0907)

Kitchen staff in the Boarding House Kitchen, West Side, at the Treadwell Mine. (Alaska State Library, Case and Draper Photographs, Photographers: Case & Draper, ASL-P39-0900)

East-Side Boarding House Kitchen staff. (Alaska State Library, Case and Draper Photographs, Photographers: Case & Draper, ASL-P39-329)

Death of an Empire - Collapse of the Treadwell Gold Mine: A Pictorial History Book

Mine workers with picks and other mining equipment in 1908. (Alaska State Library, William R. Norton Photography Collection, Photographer: William Howard Case, ASL-P226-336)

Workers at Treadwell in 1908. (Alaska State Library, William R. Norton Photography Collection, Photographer: William Howard Case, ASL-P226-335)

Miners at Treadwell in 1908. (Alaska State Library, William R. Norton Photography Collection, Photographer: William Howard Case, ASL-P226-337)

The Ready Bullion Team Co. #1 during the July 4th hose race in 1908. (Alaska State Library, William R. Norton Photography Collection, Photographer: William Howard Case, ASL-P226-303)

The staff at the Treadwell Boarding House main dining room, July 4, 1908. (Alaska State Library, William R. Norton Photography Collection, Photographer: William Howard Case, ASL-P226-326)

Workers seated for a meal at the Treadwell Boarding House main dining room, July 4, 1908.
(Alaska State Library, William R. Norton Photography Collection, Photographer: William Howard Case, ASL-P226-327)

Exhibit illustrating production of the Treadwell Mines tonnage and value annually from 1885-1904 with total value of $21.8 million. In contrast, Treadwell Mine Superintendent Joseph C. MacDonald, and another man, stand next to a cube inscribed that only $7.2 million was paid for Alaska. (Alaska State Library, Winter and Pond Photographs, Photographers: Winter and Pond, ASL-P87-0385)

Chapter Four – Death of the Empire

One fateful day in April 1917;

When the icy waters of Gastineau spilled in;

The mighty Treadwell, 700, and Mexican Mines then flooded;

It was as if God's mighty voice had violently uttered;

You'll steal the Earth's ore no more from within;

Homes and buildings then shifted or fell in;

Treadwell once king in ruins to see;

The reign of the mighty now but a memory.

♦♦♦ *Kevin Lee McIver, 2013*

The Ready Bullion Mine bulkhead, ca. 1917. Numerous cave-ins occurred during 1916-1917 in the upper levels of the mines. To protect the Treadwell, Mexican, and 700 Mines, a bulkhead was constructed that measured some 50 feet in length. The Ready Bullion Mine continued to operate for several years. (Alaska State Library, Harry F. Snyder Photograph Collection, Photographer: Harry F. Snyder, ASL-P38-041)

The Treadwell Natatorium on April 21, 1917, with the water drained as a result of the cave-in. The Natatorium was located directly over the area of the cave-in. (Alaska State Library, Harry F. Snyder Photograph Collection, Photographer: Harry F. Snyder, ASL-P38-070)

Photo of the Treadwell Mine Natatorium and the bunkhouse on April 21, 1917. Both were located directly over the cave-in area. (Alaska State Library, Harry F. Snyder Photograph Collection, Photographer: Harry F. Snyder, ASL-P38-071)

Another view of the Treadwell Mine Natatorium and the bunkhouse on April 21, 1917. All that remained the following morning after the cave-in. An exceptionally high tide caused the weakened underground workings of the 700 Mine to give away. According to the album, the surface rock jammed and keyed sufficiently to hold while the tide ebbed, saving Treadwell from a tragic disaster. (Alaska State Library, Harry F. Snyder Photograph Collection, Photographer: Harry F. Snyder, ASL-P38-068)

April 22, 1917 after the Treadwell, 700 Mine, and Mexican Mines were flooded. The building air pressure exploded the Mexican shaft house, but the Ready Bullion Mine was protected by a newly-constructed bulkhead, enabling mining operations to continue in the 1940s. (Alaska State Library, Harry F. Snyder Photograph Collection, Photographer: Harry F. Snyder, ASL-P38-072)

View from the brink of the cave-in on the morning of April 22, 1917. Debris from the natatorium building, along with tailings from the 700 Mill, were washed away by subsequent tides. (Alaska State Library, Harry F. Snyder Photograph Collection, Photographer: Harry F. Snyder, ASL-P38-074)

The ruptured fuel tank and boiler house can be seen in this photo of from April 22, 1917. The Treadwell Club is visible to the right and the house on the hill is a company-owned family house. (Alaska State Library, Harry F. Snyder Photograph Collection, Photographer: Harry F. Snyder, ASL-P38-079)

According to the album, soon after this photograph was taken, the house on the upper right, collapsed into the hole. The same fate already occurred to the natatorium building and the fuel oil tank. (Alaska State Library, Harry F. Snyder Photograph Collection, Photographer: Harry F. Snyder, ASL-P38-075)

View from the water of the bluff above the cave-in, ca. 1917. (Alaska State Library, Harry F. Snyder Photograph Collection, Photographer: Harry F. Snyder, ASL-P38-090)

The Treadwell store and office after the fire of Oct. 10, 1926. (Alaska State Library, Alaska State Library Place File, Photographers: Winter & Pond, ASL-Treadwell-Fire-01)

Chapter Five – Treadwell Today

Only remnants remain of the glorious past;

Decaying structures are all that last;

Gold in abundance a half-mile below;

Unreachable due to man's character exposed;

A love for only the color of the yellow rock;

Treadwell so sad stands a case to mock.

♦ ♦ ♦ *Kevin Lee McIver, 2013*

Marker at the Treadwell Mine site reading, "This commemorative marker is placed on the site of the Treadwell Town Plaza and on the site of the now-filled cove at the mouth of Paris Creek where gold was first found on Douglas Island. (Photo: Kevin Lee McIver)

Higher on this creek at a place later lost to Glory Hole Mining the Treadwell lode was discovered and staked in May of 1881. This was first developed and mined by John Treadwell 1882-1889 then was worked by the Alaska Treadwell Gold Mining Company and affiliates until finally closed in 1922.

F.W. Bradley of San Francisco headed all work 1899-1922. His superintendents included R.A. Kinzie, P. Bradley, R.G. Wayland, and L.M. Metzgar. Geologists were D.H. Hershey and Livingston Wernecke.

Shaft depth reached more than 2800 feet. Five mills dropped 960 stamps. Gold production totaled some 3.3 million ounces. Daily payroll long exceeded more than a 1,000 men. Life here was good." (Photo: Kevin Lee McIver)

Today, Treadwell ruins are a popular place for hikers and dog walkers. (Photo: Kevin Lee McIver)

Pilings that once supported the great Treadwell mine infrastructure now stand decaying along the beach looking toward Juneau in the distance. (Photo: Kevin Lee McIver)

Rising out of the high tide of the Gastineau Channel, the salt water pump stationed carried in needed water to support mining operations when water from the mountain above Treadwell was not in supply. [9](Photo: Kevin Lee McIver)

---

[9] City and Borough of Juneau, Parks and Recreation, "History of the Treadwell Mines Alaska," <http://www.juneau.org/parkrec/museum/HTM/Treadwellmine/qt/qfeature10.htm>.

Salt water pump marker on the trail. (Photo: Kevin Lee McIver)

Another view of the salt water pump looking south along Sandy Beach at low tide. (Photo: Kevin Lee McIver)

Treadwell Mining Company office building marker. (Photo: Kevin Lee McIver)

All that remains of the once great mining empire is the shell of the office building. (Photo: Kevin Lee McIver)

Achtung Minen! English translation, Warning Mine! Painted on the wall of the office building.
(Photo: Kevin Lee McIver)

Looking inside the two-story office building now covered in graffiti. (Photo: Kevin Lee McIver)

Another view inside the office building. The old heater is located just inside and stands as a reminder that this was once a modern building with heat and electricity. (Photo: Kevin Lee McIver)

Close up photograph of the heater. (Photo: Kevin Lee McIver)

An ornate radiator heater, just one of the many artifacts littering the area. (Photo: Kevin Lee McIver)

View above the cave-in site looking from Douglas Island toward Thane, just south of Juneau. The long white line of snow coming down was the aftermath of an avalanche that happened a month or two before this was taken. (Photo: Kevin Lee McIver)

Another view of above the cave-in area. (Photo: Kevin Lee McIver)

Site of the once grand superintendent's house that is now void of structures. Nature has regained this area and trees grow where the magnificent house once stood. (Photo: Kevin Lee McIver)

Looking along the trail. Gastineau Channel can be seen through the trees. (Photo: Kevin Lee McIver)

Walking along the Treadwell Trail or along Sandy Beach is a glimpse into the past. At every step and turn rusted pieces of machinery and cables are visible. (Photo: Kevin Lee McIver)

Death of an Empire - Collapse of the Treadwell Gold Mine: A Pictorial History Book

Move evidence of this once great mining operation. (Photo: Kevin Lee McIver)

The original stamp mill used by John Treadwell. The stamps crushed the ore as part of the extraction process. This stands in testament of the advanced mining operations at that time and today marks the entrance to the trail along Sandy Beach (to the left). [10] (Photo: Kevin Lee McIver)

---

[10] City and Borough of Juneau, Parks and Recreation, "History of the Treadwell Mines Alaska," <http://www.juneau.org/parkrec/museum/HTM/Treadwellmine/qt/qfeature4.htm>.

Cable littering the Treadwell mine area on Douglas Island. (Photo: Kevin Lee McIver)

Site of the 300 Mill, which was the largest stamp mil in the world in its time, where concrete foundations are still visible. Before the cave-in in 1917, five separate mills with a total of 960 stamps were crushing ore from four separate mines.[11] (Photo: Kevin Lee McIver)

---

[11] City and Borough of Juneau, Parks and Recreation, "History of the Treadwell Mines Alaska," <http://www.juneau.org/parkrec/museum/HTM/Treadwellmine/qt/qfeature6.htm>.

Another area were concrete structures can be seen is where the steam plant once stood.
(Photo: Kevin Lee McIver)

As you walk along the trail, the steam plant is one of the first structures encountered. Covered in vegetation, it is reminisce of ancient ruins except the end of the Treadwell era occurred less than 100 years ago. (Photo: Kevin Lee McIver)

The steam plant from the other side. (Photo: Kevin Lee McIver)

The power room can be seen above the steam plant. (Photo: Kevin Lee McIver)

The Power Room, which stands above the steam plant structure, is one of the few remaining buildings at the mine complex. (Photo: Kevin Lee McIver)

Although little evidence remains of much of the mine complex, it is interesting to note that during its heyday, the Treadwell Mine complex was complete with modern conveniences like tennis courts and a bowling alley. (Photo: Kevin Lee McIver)

*At many points pilings are visible that once supported piers and buildings occupying the **Treadwell Mine Complex.*** (Photo: Kevin Lee McIver)

Rails from the train that transported the ore. Although difficult to see, you can make out the rails below the vegetation. (Photo: Kevin Lee McIver)

One of the carts that transported the ore via the rail tracks in the previous photograph.
(Photo: Kevin Lee McIver)

Water pipe seen from the trail. The pipes transported water that was used for the stamp-mill process. [12] (Photo: Kevin Lee McIver)

---

[12] City and Borough of Juneau, Parks and Recreation, "History of the Treadwell Mines Alaska," http://www.juneau.org/parkrec/museum/HTM/Treadwellmine/qt/qfeature10.htm.

Looking north from the end of the old Treadwell Mine Complex on Douglas Island. Tailings from the mine, machinery, broken china, engine parts, bathroom tiles, and other debris litter the waterfront. (Photo: Kevin Lee McIver)

Another close up of debris lining the beach along the Treadwell Mine. (Photo: Kevin Lee McIver)

Traveling to Alaska or interested in visiting the Last Frontier?

Interested in visiting Alaska? You can find an abundant amount of information about traveling to Alaska at GroovyOutdoors.us

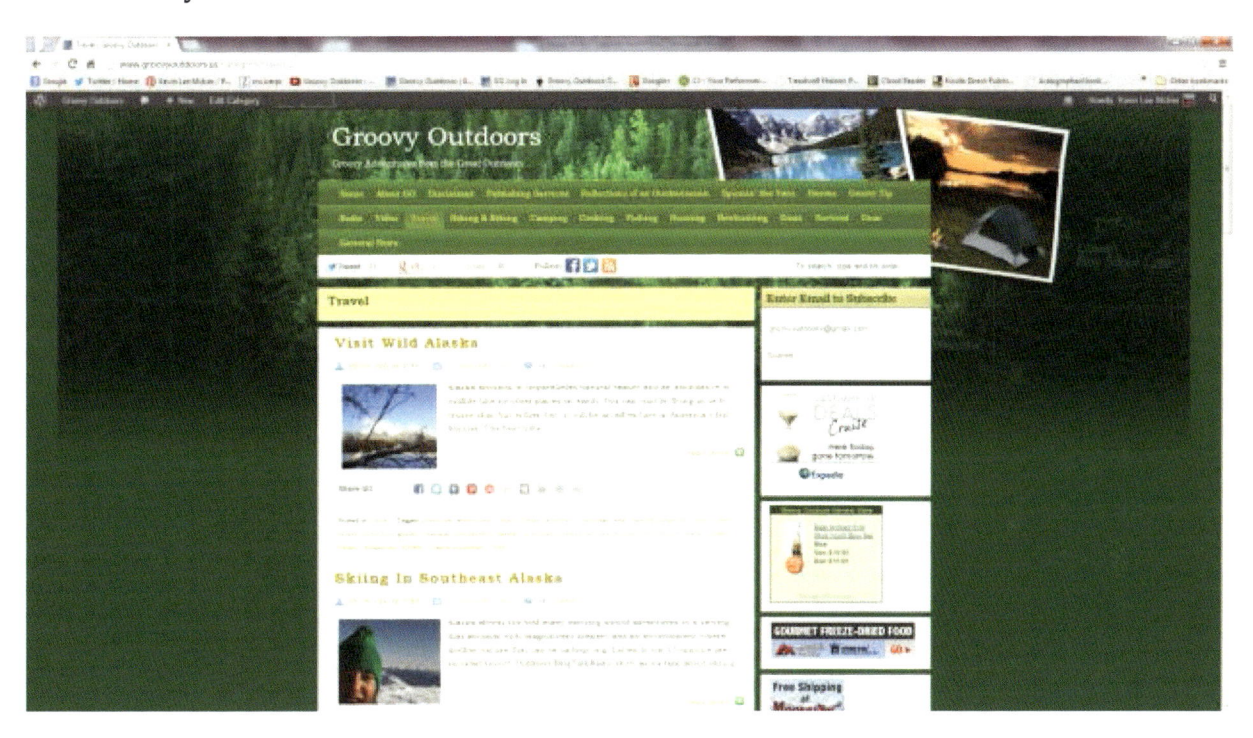

Acknowledgments

My heartfelt appreciation to all those public and private organizations that make this historical information available to the world:

Alaska Digital Archives (http://vilda.alaska.edu/cdm/index)

Alaska Light and Power Company (http://www.aelp.com/)

Library of Congress (http://www.loc.gov/)

Southern Methodist University-Central University Libraries (http://smu.edu/cul/index.html)

State of Alaska (http://alaska.gov/)

The Alaska State Library (http://www.library.state.ak.us/)

The City and Borough of Juneau (http://www.juneau.org)

The Juneau Empire (http://juneauempire.com/)

Trail Mix, Inc. (http://www.juneautrails.org/)

Treadwell Historic Preservation & Restoration Society, Inc. (http://www.treadwellsociety.com/)

About the Author

Kevin's unabashed obsession with the English language is only rivaled by his unparalleled drive to enmesh himself with technology and the great outdoors. Hunting, fishing, and living in the great outdoors are etched in his soul.

An avid outdoorsman, he has lived in Europe, the Middle East, and Asia—and draws much of his creative ideas from time spent as an Army special operations Soldier, Paratrooper, and Ranger.

From blasting out of a UH-1H helicopter at 3,000 feet, to sleeping in a snow cave in the Italian Alps, Kevin lives the Ranger Creed and by a set of time-tested Army values handed down through a distinguished lineage of Soldiers—Rangers Lead the Way!

Today, Kevin lives in South Carolina where he writes novels, poetry, and historical pieces.

Bibliography

City and Borough of Juneau, Parks and Recreation, "History of the Treadwell Mines Alaska," <http://www.juneau.org/parkrec/museum/HTM/Treadwellmine/no/xfeature1.htm>. Also:

- ❖ http://www.juneau.org/parkrec/museum/HTM/Treadwellmine/qt/qfeature4.htm.
- ❖ http://www.juneau.org/parkrec/museum/HTM/Treadwellmine/qt/qfeature6.htm.
- ❖ http://www.juneau.org/parkrec/museum/HTM/Treadwellmine/qt/qfeature10.htm.

Houdek, Jennifer, "Treadwell Gold Mines, 1881-1917," <http://www.litsite.org/index.cfm?section=Digital-Archives&page=Industry&cat=Mining&viewpost=2&ContentId=2743>.

Kelly, Sheila, "Treadwell Gold, An Alaska Saga of Riches and Ruin." University of Alaska Press, 2011. <http://www.alaska.edu/uapress/browse/detail/index.xml?id=389 and www.treadwellgold.com>.

Stone, David and Brenda, "Golden Places, The History of Alaska-Yukon Mining," <http://www.nps.gov/history/history/online_books/yuch/golden_places/chap7.htm#1> (1980).

The Full Wiki, "Gold Mining in Alaska, Historical lode and placer gold mines, Juneau Mining District," <http://www.thefullwiki.org/Juneau_mining_district>.

Triposo, "Treadwell gold mine," <https://www.triposo.com/poi/N__1006702752>.

Wikipedia, "Treadwell Gold Mine", <http://en.wikipedia.org/wiki/Treadwell_gold_mine>.

Made in the USA
Lexington, KY
22 September 2013